g to share

MOVE OVER!

LEARNING TO SHARE OUR SPACE

By Janine Amos and Annabel Spenceley
Consultant Rachael Underwood

Published in the United States by Windmill Books (Alphabet Soup)
Windmill Books
303 Park Avenue South
Suite #1280
New York, NY 10010-3657

U.S. publication copyright ©Evans Brothers Limited 2009
First North American Edition

Library of Congress Cataloging-in-Publication Data

      Amos, Janine
Move over! : learning to share our space / by Janine Amos and Annabel Spenceley.
      p.   cm. – (Best behavior)
      Contents: The tent—The rocket.
      Summary: Two brief stories demonstrate that people can feel cramped and angry
when they do not have enough space, and the importance of looking for more space when it
is needed.
      ISBN 978-1-60754-029-8 (lib.) – 978-1-60754-050-2 (pbk.)
978-1-60754-051-9 (6 pack)
      1. Social interaction in children—Juvenile literature   2. Problem solving in
children—Juvenile literature [1. Problem solving 2. Behavior   3. Etiquette
4. Conduct of life] I. Spenceley, Annabel II. Title III. Series
      177'.1—dc22

American Library Binding 13-digit ISBN: 978-1-60754-029-8
Paperback 13-digit ISBN: 978-1-60754-050-2
6 pack 13-Digit ISBN: 978-1-60754-051-9

Manufactured in China

Credits:
Editor: Louise John
Designer: D.R. Ink
Photography: Gareth Boden
Production: Jenny Mulvanney

With thanks to our models:
Amelia John, Elizabeth and Grace Walsingham, Charley Winter, Sophie and Alistair
Gleghorn, Callum Palmer, Carl Robertson, and Luke Reynolds.

The Tent

Amelia is playing in the tent.

Here comes
Elizabeth.

Amelia and Elizabeth are in the tent.

Here come Grace and Charley.

Amelia, Elizabeth, Grace, and Charley are all in the tent.

Here comes Sophie.

Sophie squeezes into the tent.

How do the others feel?

"Move over!"
grumbles Charley.
"I'm squashed."

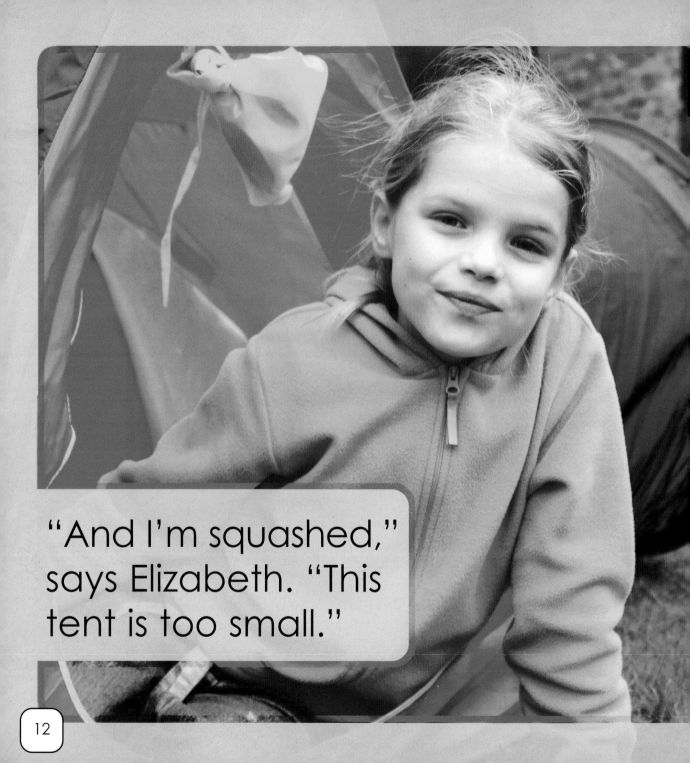

"And I'm squashed," says Elizabeth. "This tent is too small."

Elizabeth crawls out.

Elizabeth gets two chairs.

"I need this rug," she says.
"Help me, Sophie."

Elizabeth and Sophie make another tent.

Now there's room
for everyone.

Oh dear!
Here comes Alistair.

The Rocket

The table is covered with boxes. Callum is building a rocket.

"Hey! Move over! I need more space," says Carl.

"Zoom! Zoom!"
goes Callum.

"Move over!" shouts Carl. He pushes the boxes on to the floor.

"What's going on here?" asks Luke.
"You two look upset."

"Carl pushed my boxes," says Callum.

25

"He's taking up all the table. There's no room for me," says Carl.

"So you both need more space," says Luke. "What can we do?"

"I've got a good idea," says Callum. "I could build my rocket upward."

"Show me!" says Luke. Callum holds his rocket up.

"Look! There's space for me now!" smiles Carl.

Callum finishes his rocket.
And Carl makes his space buggy.

FOR FURTHER READING

INFORMATION BOOKS

Krasny Brown, Laurie. *How to Be a Friend: a Guide to Making Friends and Keeping Them*. Boston: Little, Brown Young Readers, 2001.

Mattern, Joanne. *Do You Help Others*? New York: Weekly Reader Early Learning Library, 2007.

FICTION

Grindley, Sally. *The Big What Are Friends For*? *Storybook*. New York: Kingfisher, 2002.

AUTHOR BIO
Janine has worked in publishing as an editor and author, as a lecturer in education. Her interests are in personal growth and raising self-esteem and she works with educators, child psychologists and specialists in mediation. She has written more than fifty books for children. Many of her titles deal with first time experiences and emotional health issues such as Bullying, Death, and Divorce.

You can find more great fiction and nonfiction from Windmill Books at windmillbks.com